★★★★★★★★★★★★★★★★★★

NITRO CIRCUS

T0105954

BEST OF
RALLYCROSS

RIPLEY
PUBLISHING
a Jim Pattison Company

WHAT IS RALLYCROSS?

LIKE MOTOCROSS RACING ON FOUR WHEELS!

Before talking rallycross, you must first understand its roots in rally racing. Rally racing consists of street-legal cars racing one at a time on a public road—that's closed for racing, of course. Each race, or stage, is timed, and drivers and their co-drivers (or navigators) must traverse all kinds of terrain (i.e., gravel, snow, etc.).

Rallycross evolved from rally. A sprint auto racing on a closed circuit with specially modified cars, it takes the most exciting elements from stage rally and brings them into an exciting head-to-head environment where the fans can see all the action from a single location.

It's an action sport that couples mixed-surface car racing with fantastic jumps and banked berms. Rallycross cars typically have all-wheel drive to handle the dirt course and off-road style suspension, which is best for long jumps.

Rallycross enjoyed popularity primarily in Europe until it was added to the X Games in 2010, where it was called SuperRally. In 2011, rallycross got another boost in the United States with the Global Rallycross Championship, where riders could hone their skills and expose the sport to a wider audience.

In 2018, Nitro added rallycross to its long list of action sports. Travis Pastrana and crew built a custom track with multiple racing lines and some of the biggest jumps and berms ever attempted on a rallycross track! Nitro Rallycross features many big names from the sport, including Nitro's own Travis Pastrana.

WRC
FIA WORLD RALLY
CHAMPIONSHIP

KEY FACTS

The average value of a WRC car is around $1 million!

- - - - - - - - - - - - - - - - - -

Each rally is split into 15 to 25 special stages, which are run against the clock on closed roads.

- - - - - - - - - - - - - - - - - -

An average day consists of 250 miles of driving!

- - - - - - - - - - - - - - - - - -

The WRC rallies currently take place all around Europe, and even in Argentina, Japan, Kenya, Mexico, and New Zealand.

SARDEGNA
endless islar

WORLD RALLY CHAMPIONSHIP

THE HIGHEST CLASS OF INTERNATIONAL RALLYING

The FIA WRC is a rallying series in its 47th year that takes place mainly in Europe. It involves 14 three-day races on all kinds of challenging terrain, including gravel, tarmac, snow, and even ice!

The "special" stages are driven on closed roads. They are connected by non-competitive sections— open roads where drivers must obey the country's road laws. Based on points earned at these rallies, which take place throughout the calendar year, the WRC awards a champion driver, co-driver, and manufacturer. Believe it or not, they aren't always from the same team!

DID YOU KNOW?

World Rally cars must be built to follow WRC regulations. They are production 1.6-liter four-cylinder cars but also include many enhancements, like turbochargers, anti-lag systems, four-wheel drive, sequential gearboxes, and aerodynamic design elements.

GRAVEL

WRC
FIA WORLD RALLY
CHAMPIONSHIP

KEY FACTS

The maximum total distance of the special stages was lowered to 217.5 miles in 2019.

Surfaces such as ice, snow, gravel, and tarmac are common.

Some special stages include rough forest tracks into mountainous territories.

During the special stages, drivers can't get help from their teams. They have to deal with breakdowns or other problems themselves.

WORLD RALLY CHAMPIONSHIP STAGES

CHALLENGING TERRAIN, SOLITARY RACES

The WRC's 14 races take place on all kinds of terrain, including gravel, tarmac, snow, and ice. Each rally event is split into 15 to 25 special stages, which are run against the clock on closed roads. The driver with the lowest overall time wins the event (and the maximum number of points).

Each racer begins the stage after a set interval. This is usually two minutes. Pacing out the drivers reduces the chance of interference. Each special stage is pretty short—usually a max of 30 miles.

TARMAC

RALLY ON ICE AND SNOW

WHERE SLIDING BECOMES ART

The terrain of the special stages varies greatly, depending a lot on the country in which it's held.

Nordic countries typically include stages with ice or snow.

Ott Tanäk of Estonia and Martin Järveoja of Estonia celebrate their victory on the final podium during Day Three of the WRC Sweden on February 17, 2019, in Torsby, Sweden.

DID YOU KNOW?

Racing on ice and snow is all about controlling the slide—shifting and breaking as needed to maximize the speed and control over these slick surfaces. The lighter car guarantees the slide but ups the challenge of maintaining control.

WORLD RALLYCROSS CHAMPIONSHIP

INTERNATIONAL RALLYCROSS AT ITS BEST

The FIA World Rallycross Championship series, born in 2014, includes 12 two-day racing events that are driven on closed circuits with mixed surfaces (mostly asphalt and gravel).

Each event has four qualifying heats, two semi-finals, and a final. Drivers earn points from their placement in each event. Based on their overall points at the end of the season, the World RX awards a champion driver and team.

Swede Johan David Kristoffersson won back-to-back World RX titles in 2017 and 2018. During the 2018 season, he enjoyed a record-breaking 11 event wins.

Two classes of cars currently run in World RX—Supercar and RX2 (also called Supercar Lites). There is work underway to add a fully electric car category soon.

FIA WORLD
RALLYCROSS
CHAMPIONSHIP

TRADITIONAL WORLD RX COURSES

SHORT BOUTS OF AGGRESSIVE EXCITEMENT!

The World RX courses boast several different kinds of surfaces, including asphalt, dirt, and sometimes gravel. They always include a jump or two, but watch out for that joker lap! That's where strategy comes into play.

Courses are also very short—sometimes even less than one minute for the Supercars to finish. Rallycross is perfect for those with short attention spans!

PIT TALK

The joker lap is a standard feature of rallycross courses. Each course has a standard route and a joker lap. Drivers must take the joker lap once during the race. Usually, it's longer than the main route, but in some championships, it's longer *and* has more obstacles. The driver has to strategize when it's best to take the joker lap to maximize his or her time on the course.

RX FIA WORLD RALLYCROSS CHAMPIONSHIP

KEY FACTS

Drivers get just 12 laps of practice.

Drivers compete in four rounds of qualifying heats and accumulate points in each.

Each qualifying run is a four-lap race with three to six cars fighting for the best total time.

If a driver doesn't run the joker lap, he or she gets a 30-second penalty.

FROM ASPHALT TO GRAVEL

DRIVERS HAVE TO BE READY FOR IT ALL

The World RX courses include all kinds of wild terrain, depending on when and where they are held.

Drivers have to be ready for anything. They may adopt different shifting and braking skills but must use regulation tires on all vehicles.

Here, Norway driver Andreas Mikkelsen and his co-driver Anders Jæner drive a Hyundai i20 Coupe WRC during the first day of RallyRACC Catalunya-Costa Daurada, on October 26, 2018.

RX FIA WORLD RALLYCROSS CHAMPIONSHIP

▨KEY FACTS▨

The races in Sweden and Norway usually run in the middle of the summer.

Laps may be run in sandy desert conditions.

Gravel, a more common surface, presents challenges in terms of drifting. Drivers use sliding and traction to their benefit. With the right tires and skills, they can drift around turns and berms and take seconds off their time.

ASPHALT

NITRO RALLYCROSS

RALLYCROSS GETS THE NITRO WORLD GAMES TREATMENT

In 2018, Nitro World Games welcomed rallycross into its action sports fold. Heading up the action was Travis Pastrana, rally driver, action sports veteran, and Nitro Circus co-founder.

The idea was to turn the sport of rallycross on its head and create a permanent course that puts the race back in the drivers' hands.

Pastrana called Nitro's permanent rallycross track a "hell track for cars," since the track has more of everything that makes the race challenging.

At the inaugural Nitro Rallycross two-day event in 2018, nine of the top rally drivers in the world competed to become the first-ever NRX champion. Timmy Hansen took home the victory, with Mattias Ekström in 2nd and Tanner Foust in 3rd.

Tanner Foust

Timmy Hansen

Mattias Ekström

"Rallycross is where all the action sports motorheads eventually end up. Drifting sideways and flying through the air brings in all the elements of excitement we are used to from our childhood—only faster and less physically demanding on our broken bodies."
—*Travis Pastrana*

Travis Pastrana on NRX:
"Typical rallycross is fun. But Nitro Rallycross is going to take the sport to another level of excitement for the drivers and our fans."

YOKOHAMA®

NRX AT THE NITRO WORLD GAMES 2019

NITRO BRINGS RALLYCROSS TO THE NEXT LEVEL!

The 2019 Nitro Rallycross event, held at Nitro's Utah Motorsports Campus, built on the progression of the first event, with more world-class drivers, a more challenging and fine-tuned course, and the largest jump ever in a rallycross race.

The goal is always to push the limits of what is conceivable and possible.

Believe it or not, all three drivers who stood atop the podium in 2019 are Swedish, and Kevin and Timmy are brothers.

Patrik Sandell

Kevin Hansen

Timmy Hansen

In 2019, it was Kevin Hansen who stood on top of the podium—the only driver in the NRX championship race who didn't enter the previous year. His brother Timmy Hansen, the 2018 champion, took 3rd. Patrik Sandell took 2nd place.

UTAH SPORTS COMMISSION®

THE NRX COURSE

MORE OF EVERYTHING YOU LOVE ABOUT RALLYCROSS

Nitro's permanent rallycross course, built in 2018 at the Utah Motor Sports Campus, starts straight off into a jump! This track has more dirt sections, more obstacles, more sliding and passing opportunities, and some of the largest jumps and berms ever seen on a rallycross track.

With many options to take larger or smaller jumps and left or right berms, the idea is to put the race more in the driver's hands, based on the decisions he or she makes.

NRX
NITRO RALLYCROSS

KEY FACTS

NRX boasts the largest man-made jump in rallycross history!

The permanent track, according to Pastrana, "allows us testing time to dial it all in."

The joker lap is about two seconds slower than the main lap.

PIT TALK

A **berm** is a steep, curved barrier made of dirt or soil that helps drivers take a corner at speed. The NRX course is full of strategically placed berms to make the rally more exciting and keep the speeds quick!

SUPERCARS

RALLYCROSS CARS

UNMATCHED SPEED AND AGILITY

Rallycross cars fall into several categories, depending on what the driver needs from his or her machine.

You can bet they all excel at speed and agility. The cars in the Supercar class can accelerate from 0 to 60 mph in 1.9 seconds—that's faster than a Formula 1 car!

These **Supercars** are hatchbacks turned into the ultimate racing beasts by adding turbocharged, two-liter, 600-brake horsepower engines and four-wheel drive. Models include the Subaru WRX, Ford Fiesta, Peugeot 208, Volkswagen Polo (on the WRX side), Volkswagen Beetle (on the American side), and of course, the Mini Cooper.

The **RX2 Supercar Lite** is a special category with 310-brake horsepower, mid-engined (mounted in the middle of the car for best performance), four-wheel drive. Just like the Supercars, RX2 machines have a six-speed sequential gearbox. They provide a great learning ground for aspiring Supercar drivers, and did so for the likes of Kevin Hansen.

TOURING

The **Touring car** has rear-wheel drive and a two-liter engine. This modern interpretation of traditional rallycross cars has been a good first step for future Supercar drivers. Many past champions have progressed to the Supercar category.

SUPER 1600

DID YOU KNOW?

Four drivers competed in Subaru WRX STI rallycross cars at the 2019 Nitro World Games' Nitro Rallycross (NRX) event, including Travis Pastrana, Scott Speed, Patrik Sandell, and Chris Atkinson.

These **Super 1600** cars are front-wheel-drive hatchbacks with 1600cc engines. This is where many of the top Supercar drivers have developed, including Sébastien Loeb. These cars give young drivers an entry point into professional rallying.

RALLY CAR DESIGN

BUILT FOR HEAVY-DUTY ABUSE

Cars used in rally and rallycross are different. Rallycross cars have fewer engine restrictions and do not have to be street legal.

The basic rally car design is a standard hatchback, modified to take abuse over long hours of driving and rough roads.

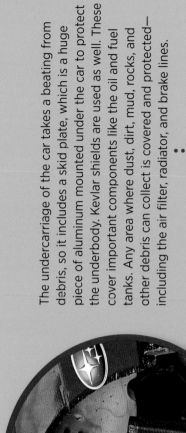

The undercarriage of the car takes a beating from debris, so it includes a skid plate, which is a huge piece of aluminum mounted under the car to protect the underbody. Kevlar shields are used as well. These cover important components like the oil and fuel tanks. Any area where dust, dirt, mud, rocks, and other debris can collect is covered and protected—including the air filter, radiator, and brake lines.

Heavy-duty suspension is critical to a rally car. They need robust shock absorbers and springs to absorb the dirty, rocky, sandy, snowy conditions they race in.

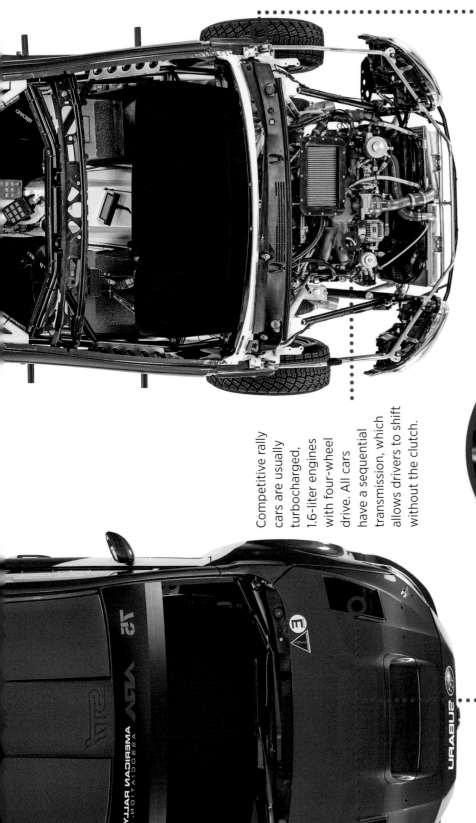

Brakes are very important in rally racing. The winner is often the driver who comes *out of* a turn or corner the fastest. Those who do the opposite and are fastest *into* the corner often struggle for speed. The brakes need to be able to handle all that wear!

Competitive rally cars are usually turbocharged, 1.6-liter engines with four-wheel drive. All cars have a sequential transmission, which allows drivers to shift without the clutch.

Aerodynamic elements are added to the body, including rear wings for downforce, vents above the engine to allow heat to leave the bay, and air scoops on the roof to provide cooling and positive air flow in the cabin.

INSIDE THE RALLYCROSS CAR

COCKPIT COMMAND CONTROL

The cockpit is where all the magic happens.

Different cars have different setups, but you can rest assured they all have these basic controls placed perfectly for quick access.

The driver's dash display shows lots of important information, including what gear the driver is in, the RPMs, other vital engine info, and any special modes the car can accommodate. It's information that's central for the driver.

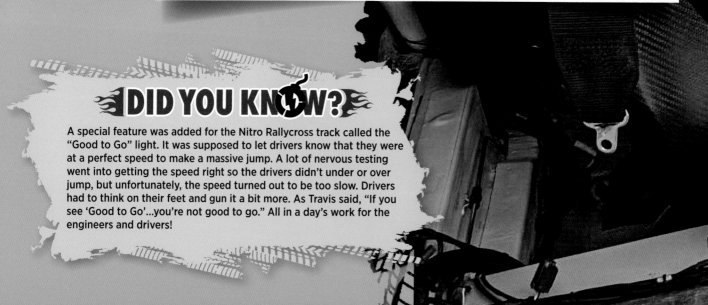

DID YOU KNOW?

A special feature was added for the Nitro Rallycross track called the "Good to Go" light. It was supposed to let drivers know that they were at a perfect speed to make a massive jump. A lot of nervous testing went into getting the speed right so the drivers didn't under or over jump, but unfortunately, the speed turned out to be too slow. Drivers had to think on their feet and gun it a bit more. As Travis said, "If you see 'Good to Go'...you're not good to go." All in a day's work for the engineers and drivers!

hifting gears is a constant, strategically motivated ction while racing through the various laps. Drivers eed a convenient way to shift gears.

Professional rallycross cars also have buttons and dials for various controls. These are often situated right in the middle of the steering wheel. Performance buttons include Launch Control (for turbo boost). You'll also find normal controls here, like wipers and radio communication.

The handbrake is a hydraulic system controlled by the driver and only acts on the rear wheels. When the driver pulls the handbrake lever, it simultaneously disconnects the drive shaft to the rear of the car and applies pressure to the rear brakes only. If the system did not disconnect the driveshaft, the forces applied to lock the rear brakes would stall the engine.

INSIDE THE CAR
KEY FACTS

All racecars have fire suppression systems within the cockpit, usually under the seat.

The external kill switch kills all electrical power to the car in the event of a fire or other mishap. That switch must be accessible to the driver from the inside, too.

Maybe the most important safety feature of all rallycross cars is the six-point roll cage inside the cockpit. It runs along the inside of the chassis and helps stiffen the car to provide safety during rolls and flips.

TIRES FOR ALL TERRAINS

HEAVY-DUTY RALLYCROSS CAR TIRES

Rallycross tires are specially made to handle the turns, skids, and accelerations of a rallycross race.

The edges of tires have a hard ridge instead of being rounded like road tires, which gives drivers better lateral grip.

This much thicker area around the beading of the tire helps avoid flats and protects the edge of wheel.

![NRX NITRO RALLYCROSS PASTRANA YOKOHAMA]

DID YOU KNOW?

Softer rubber compounds are used for colder climates and harder ones for warmer climates. The harder the rubber, the better the tire wears and the longer it lasts. Rallycross drivers are willing to sacrifice tire life for better handling and grip.

TIRES
⬛KEY FACTS⬛

Rallycross tires are wider, with Kevlar instead of steel belting in the tread, to give them more flexibility on various surfaces.

The sidewall is stiffer and contains steel belting, for best results around berms and slides.

In rallycross, drivers are not allowed to have traction control, electronic stability control, or antilock braking.

The rubber compounds used in rallycross cars are usually softer, which is better for gripping gravel and icy roads.

The balaclava is a ski-mask-type cap that drivers wear under their helmets. It is flame resistant and heat protective.

PIT TALK

A **HANS** device is a Head and Neck Support device that attaches to the back of the helmet. It's an added safety measure in the event of a severe crash, because a heavy helmet can injure your neck and spine during a roll or flip of the car.

The shirt, pants, overalls, gloves, and socks that professional drivers wear are flame resistant and have heat protection against direct flame contact and radiant heat. They give drivers a good 20 seconds to escape a fire without being burned.

HELMET KEY FACTS

The FIA standard helmet has impact protection that's equivalent to a free fall from 15 feet.

It has debris penetration protection equivalent to being struck by a 8-pound object being dropped from 10 feet.

The helmets also have a frontal head restraint that protects drivers from neck injuries due to frontal impacts of up to 70 g.

It has flame and heat transfer protection up to 1500°F!

RALLY SAFETY GEAR

DRIVING FOR THE LONG RUN

Rally drivers and the FIA are serious about their safety. Cars crash, roll, flip, and slide frequently and can even catch on fire.

These are the many ways that drivers make sure they can walk away from a potentially serious accident.

THE PIT CREW TEAM

SUPPORTING THE DRIVER AND THE CAR

The pit crew are often called the "hidden athletes of car racing."

They have to be strong and fast to pull, yank, break off, and replace parts left and right, all while racing the clock. Another word for pit crew is paddock crew.

Since rallycross truly is a contact sport, the pit crew not only tweaks car settings and changes tires between courses, but also needs to be ready to fix body damage or broken suspension components at a moment's notice.

THE PIT CREW TEAM
SUPPORTING THE DRIVER AND THE CAR

The teams are in constant communication with the drivers and always watching the car for problems.

The pit crew never has downtime.

Teams make on-the-fly adjustments to cars in between heats and stages.

F1 CARS VERSUS RALLYCROSS CARS

SPEED OR AGILITY: WHICH WINS OUT?

Many fans have wondered—if a Formula 1 car was pitted against a rallycross car, which would come out on top?

Rallycross cars in the Supercar class can accelerate from 0 to 60 mph in 1.9 seconds, which is faster than an F1 car! However, on the backstretch and straightaways, an F1 engine will eventually catch most anything.

British-born Lewis Hamilton is a six-time Formula One World Champion. Hamilton races for Mercedes and came in first in 2019 in the F1 racing standings—his third consecutive year to do so!

Lewis Hamilton

Ken Block

A tighter track gives rallycross cars the advantage because they are more agile and handle curves and turns better and more tightly. However, the monster power of an F1 car is daunting, especially with a champion at the helm.

For the Top Gear Live event in Barbados, rallycross racer Ken Block, of Gymkhana fame, went head-to-head against F1 champion Lewis Hamilton to answer this question, if not once and for all, at least once!

American Scott Speed is a multitalented driver who has competed in Formula One, NASCAR, IndyCar, Formula E, and rallycross.

He started racing American Rallycross (ARX) in 2013 and promptly won a gold medal at the X Games in Brazil in his first competitive rallycross race ever.

Team: Subaru Rally Team USA

41 Scott Speed

BORN: 01-24-83 **HOME:** Manteca, CA 🄾 @scott_speed

The first American to race in Formula One since Michael Andretti in 1993, Speed won the Global RallyCross Championship in 2015, 2016, and 2017, amassing a total of 10 wins. In 2018, he won the inaugural Americas Rallycross Championship (ARX), collecting two wins.

At the Nitro World Games in 2019, Speed fractured his vertebrae in a crash and was forced to sit out the rest of the season. At the time of his injury, he was the ARX points leader.

In his spare time, Speed loves to play golf.

Frenchman Sébastien Loeb is considered the world's most successful rally driver, having accrued a stunning nine consecutive WRC titles and 78 wins before branching out to the rallycross discipline (among others!) in recent years.

In 2019, Loeb signed to drive for Hyundai in the 2019 World Rally Championship.

Teams: Citroën, Kronos Citroën, Hyundai

19 Sebastien Loeb

BORN: 2-26-74 **HOME:** Haguenau, France @sebloebofficiel

Loeb is a three-time winner of the Race of Champions after taking home the title "Champion of Champions" in 2003, 2005, and 2008.

Because Loeb has so dominated the rally-driving world, he has been nicknamed "Le Petron," which means "the boss" in French.

He earned a gold medal at the 2012 X Games in California in rallycross.

Believe it or not, Loeb was originally a gymnast and switched to rally when he was 21.

Swede Mattias Ekström grew up with rallycross. He spent his youth learning from his dad, who competed in the European Rallycross Championship.

Ekström is the 2016 World RX Champion and two-time DTM (Deutsche Tourenwagen Masters) series title winner.

Team: EKS RX

5 Mattias Ekström

BORN: 7-14-78 **HOME:** Falun, Sweden 🅾 @mattiasekstromracing

Ekström debuted in the FIA World Rallycross Championship in 2014 and won it in 2016, but in total, he has been on the FIA World Rallycross Championship podium 22 times!

Because of the different cars and racing genres he's succeeded in over the years, he's widely regarded as one of the most versatile drivers in the world.

Ekström is also a three-time winner of the Race of Champions, an international motorsport event held at the end or start of each season, featuring some of the world's best racing and rally drivers.

Swede Timmy Hansen competes in the FIA World Rallycross Championship Supercar category.

He is the most successful rallycross driver to date, with 14 FIA European Rallycross titles to his name!

Team: Team Peugeot Total

21 Timmy Hansen

BORN: 5-21-92 **HOME:** Götene, Sweden ⓘ @timmy_hansen

Timmy Hansen is the first winner of an NRX race and the first driver to make the podium multiple races in a row.

In his first season in 2014, Hansen took one win and three podium finishes in the FIA World Rallycross Championship.

He has had four podium finishes since entering the World Rallycross Championship fray in 2012.

His interests include training, triathlons, and cooking.

The apple doesn't fall far from the tree—Hansen's father is a 14-time European Rallycross Champion, his mother is a 1994 ERA European Cup winner, and his brother Kevin is also a successful rallycross driver. It's a family affair!

Swede Kevin Hansen has managed to score six titles in four different categories and collected a total of eight silver and gold medals!

He has big shoes to fill, with his mother, father, and older brother Timmy all successful racecar drivers, but he has already paved his own path to success.

Kevin won the overall RX Lites Cup Title in 2015—pretty impressive for someone who wasn't old enough to get his regular driver's license in Sweden!

Team: Team Peugeot Total

71 Kevin Hansen

BORN: 5-28-98 **HOME:** Götene, Sweden @kevinhansen71

Kevin is the youngest ever FIA European Supercar Champion, winning the NRX race on his first attempt, in 2019.

He was the 2019 Titans RX series champion and the FIA Rookie of the Year in 2016—the same year he was the FIA European Rallycross Champion.

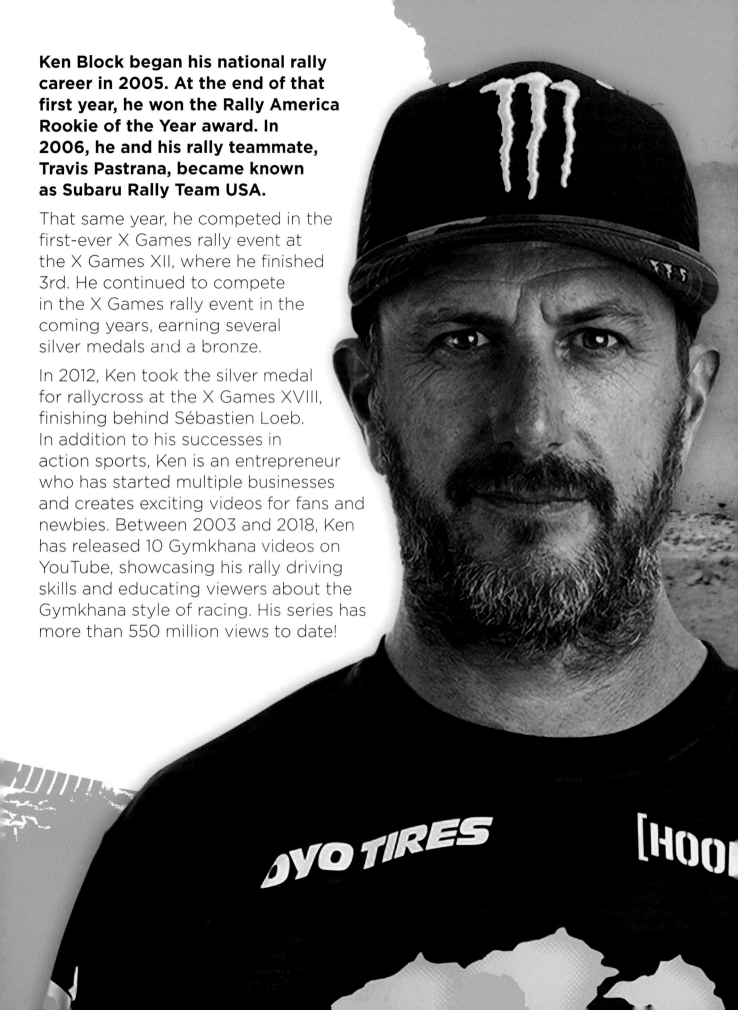

Ken Block began his national rally career in 2005. At the end of that first year, he won the Rally America Rookie of the Year award. In 2006, he and his rally teammate, Travis Pastrana, became known as Subaru Rally Team USA.

That same year, he competed in the first-ever X Games rally event at the X Games XII, where he finished 3rd. He continued to compete in the X Games rally event in the coming years, earning several silver medals and a bronze.

In 2012, Ken took the silver medal for rallycross at the X Games XVIII, finishing behind Sébastien Loeb. In addition to his successes in action sports, Ken is an entrepreneur who has started multiple businesses and creates exciting videos for fans and newbies. Between 2003 and 2018, Ken has released 10 Gymkhana videos on YouTube, showcasing his rally driving skills and educating viewers about the Gymkhana style of racing. His series has more than 550 million views to date!

Team: Hoonigan Racing Division

43 Ken Block

BORN: 11-21-67 **HOME:** Salt Lake City, UT ⑩ @kblock43

Like many of his peers, Ken has also competed in many other action sports, including skateboarding, snowboarding, and motocross.

One of the co-founders of DC Shoes, Ken also owns the business called Hoonigan Industries, which is a clothing brand for auto enthusiasts.

According to Ken and his company, a hoonigan is a person who operates a motor vehicle in an aggressive and unorthodox manner, consisting of, but not limited to, drifting, burnouts, and doughnuts, as well as acts of automotive aeronautics.

His Gymkhana videos are part of a viral series that showcases his rally driving skills.

THE GYMKHANA SERIES

KEN BLOCK'S BRAINCHILD

Rallycross driver Ken Block started recording himself while driving in order to sharpen his rally skills. The videos he posted quickly became immensely popular, so he turned his sights to sharing his passion and knowledge with others. What was born was the "Gymkhana" series of videos, which have repeatedly gone viral immediately after being posted.

The 10 Gymkhana videos on YouTube showcase Ken's rally driving skills and educate viewers about the Gymkhana style of racing. You can see them all at **www.hoonigan.com/blogs/films/gymkhana.**

Gymkhana is a type of timed/speed car racing in which drivers must get through the course as quickly as possible with the fewest mistakes. The courses usually include obstacles, like cones and barrels. The name comes from the horseback riding discipline of gymkhana.

GYMKHANA SERIES
✦KEY FACTS✦

"Gymkhana 2" was the most
viral video of 2009.

——————————————

There are 10 total episodes.
The final episode was
released in late 2018.

——————————————

More than 550 million
views to date!

——————————————

There is an Amazon series called
"The Gymkhana Files" that goes
behind the scenes of filming the
final episode, "Gymkhana 10."

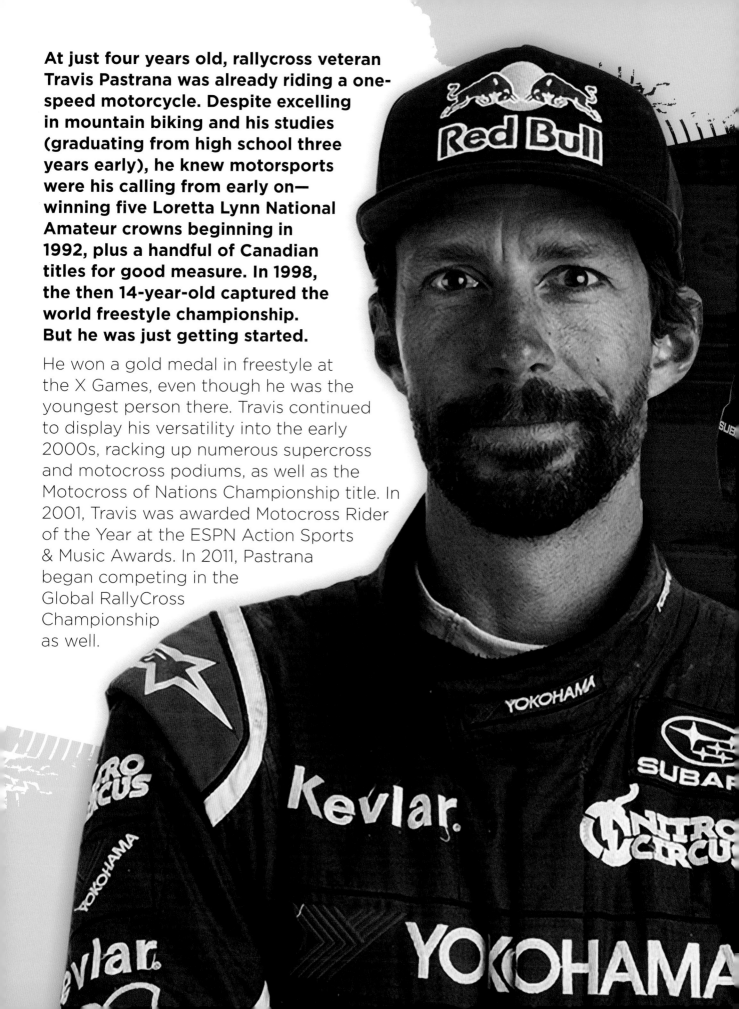

At just four years old, rallycross veteran Travis Pastrana was already riding a one-speed motorcycle. Despite excelling in mountain biking and his studies (graduating from high school three years early), he knew motorsports were his calling from early on—winning five Loretta Lynn National Amateur crowns beginning in 1992, plus a handful of Canadian titles for good measure. In 1998, the then 14-year-old captured the world freestyle championship. But he was just getting started.

He won a gold medal in freestyle at the X Games, even though he was the youngest person there. Travis continued to display his versatility into the early 2000s, racking up numerous supercross and motocross podiums, as well as the Motocross of Nations Championship title. In 2001, Travis was awarded Motocross Rider of the Year at the ESPN Action Sports & Music Awards. In 2011, Pastrana began competing in the Global RallyCross Championship as well.

Team: Subaru Motorsports USA

199 TRAVIS PASTRANA

BORN: 10-8-83 **HOME:** Annapolis, MD 🅾 @travispastrana

A rallycross veteran and its biggest fan, Travis has 17 X Games medals, including 11 gold medals, plus five golds from the Gravity Games, and more wins at other events, including Dew Tour and Red Bull X-Fighters.

As the ringleader and co-founder of Nitro Circus, Travis is committed to the progression of action sports as a whole, and that includes taking rallycross to the next level.

Travis spearheaded the layout and design of Nitro's permanent rallycross track in Utah. He designed it to have multiple racing lines and some of the biggest jumps and berms ever seen on a rallycross track.

RECORD-BREAKING RALLY CAR JUMP

NITRO'S OWN TRAVIS PASTRANA AND HIS 269-FOOT JUMP

Travis Pastrana, Nitro Circus co-founder, jumped his Subaru rally car 269 feet in the air over a ramp to set a world record!

This record-breaking jump took place on New Year's Eve 2009 in Long Beach, California, and has not been broken or even repeated since. After mastering the jump unscathed, he did a backflip off the lander, which was floating in Long Beach Harbor, into the water below, to the amazement of the crowd.

Tanner Foust was the first American driver to win a round of the European Rallycross Championship when he won the World RX of Finland in 2014.

But rallycross is just one of his many passions. He has also competed in rally, drift, and ice racing. In addition, he was a TV host for the American version of *Top Gear*.

Tanner is also a Hollywood stunt driver. He's worked in many films, including *The Need 4 Speed, The Bourne Legacy, Bourne Ultimatum, The Fast and the Furious: Tokyo Drift*, and *Iron Man 2*. He was nominated for a Taurus Stunt Award for his work on *The Fast and the Furious: Tokyo Drift*.

Team: Volkswagen Andretti Rallycross

34 Tanner Foust

BORN: 6-13-73 **HOME:** Denver, CO 🅾 @tannerfoust

You could say Tanner has a need for speed. A three-time U.S. rallycross champion, Tanner won four X Games gold medals in several different car racing categories.

He won two back-to-back Formula Drift championships in 2007 and 2008.

With nine medals, Tanner is the most decorated driver in X Games history.

Vice President, Licensing & Publishing Amanda Joiner
Editorial Manager Carrie Bolin

Editor Jessica Firpi
Designer Luis Fuentes
Text Kezia Endsley
Proofreader Rachel Paul
Reprographics Bob Prohaska

Chief Executive Officer Andy Edwards
Chief Commercial Officer Brett Clarke
Senior Vice President, Global Events Dave Mateus
Vice President, Global Licensing &
  Consumer Products Cassie Dombrowski
Vice President, Creative Dov Ribnick
Director, Brand & Athlete Marketing Ricky Melnik
Account Manager, Global Licensing &
  Consumer Products Andrew Hogan
Athlete Manager Chris Haffey
Special Thanks Travis Pastrana, Steve Arpin, Josh Tons, Chris
  Yandell, Andreas Eriksson, Subaru, Loenbro Motorsports

Published by Ripley Publishing 2020

10 9 8 7 6 5 4 3 2 1

Copyright © 2020 Nitro Circus

ISBN: 978-1-60991-388-5

For more information regarding permission, contact:
VP Licensing & Publishing
Ripley Entertainment Inc.
7576 Kingspointe Parkway, Suite 188
Orlando, Florida 32819
Email: publishing@ripleys.com
www.ripleys.com/books

Manufactured in China in March 2020.
First Printing

Library of Congress Control Number: 2020931354

PUBLISHER'S NOTE
While every effort has been made to verify the
accuracy of the entries in this book, the Publisher
cannot be held responsible for any errors contained
in the work. They would be glad to receive any
information from readers.

WARNING
Some of the stunts and activities are undertaken by
experts and should not be attempted by anyone
without adequate training and supervision.

PHOTO CREDITS